PETS' GUIDES

Henrietta's Guide to

Caring for Your Chickens

Isabel Thomas

Raintree is an imprint of Capstone Global Library Limited, a company incorporated in England and Wales having its registered office at 7 Pilgrim Street, London, EC4V 6LB – Registered company number: 6695582

www.raintreepublishers.co.uk
myorders@raintreepublishers.co.uk

Text © Capstone Global Library Limited 2015
First published in hardback in 2014
The moral rights of the proprietor have been asserted.

Edited by James Benefield and Brynn Baker
Designed by Cynthia Akiyoshi
Picture research by Tracy Cummins
Production by Victoria Fitzgerald
Originated by Capstone Global Library Limited
Printed and bound in China by RR Donnelley Asia
ISBN 978-1-406-28178-1
18 17 16 15 14
10 9 8 7 6 5 4 3 2 1

British Library Cataloguing in Publication Data
A full catalogue record for this book is available from the British Library.

Acknowledgements
We would like to thank the following for permission to reproduce photographs: Chicken School Ltd: 11, 12, 19; Getty Images: Benjamin Rondel, 7, Gary John Norman, 26, George Clerk, 9, Richard Clark, 15, Rob Whitrow, 20, Tim Graham, 22; Science Source: RIA Novosti, 25; Shutterstock: Anna Hoychuk, 17, Geanina Bechea, front cover, Melpomene, 5; Design Elements Shutterstock: iBird, Picsfive, R-studio.

We would like to thank Val Moody for her assistance in the preparation of this book.

Every effort has been made to contact copyright holders of material reproduced in this book. Any omissions will be rectified in subsequent printings if notice is given to the publisher.

All the Internet addresses (URLs) given in this book were valid at the time of going to press. However, due to the dynamic nature of the Internet, some addresses may have changed, or sites may have changed or ceased to exist since publication. While the author and publisher regret any inconvenience this may cause readers, no responsibility for any such changes can be accepted by either the author or the publisher.

Contents

Some words are shown in bold, **like this**. You can find out what they mean by looking in the glossary.

Do you want pet chickens?

Hello! I'm Henrietta and this book is all about chickens. Did you know that chickens make great pets? We're friendly and fun to watch as we explore your garden. Hens (girl chickens) even lay delicious eggs that you can eat.

Before getting pet chickens, check rules for your area. Some places don't allow you to keep chickens. Also, be sure you can look after us properly. We'll need food, water and a clean place to live. Plus, we need company and **vet** care if we get sick or injured.

Choosing your chickens

What type of chickens will suit your family? Noisy cockerels (boy chickens) may wake you and your neighbours when they crow, every morning! Most people choose to keep hens who lay nice, tasty eggs!

Baby chickens (chicks) need special care and indoor homes. Older chickens can live in almost any garden. **Breeds** of chickens come in different colours and sizes. They behave in different ways, too. If you would like lots of eggs, choose a **hybrid** like me.

Where to get chickens

Before you choose a chicken, learn all about us by visiting a farm, **breeder** or rescue centre. Choose chickens that are bright-eyed and interested in the things around them. If you choose retired **commercial hens**, they may need more care and attention.

Commercial hens lay quality eggs to sell in shops.

Get at least three chickens, because we don't like to be on our own! Ask for help to choose chickens that get along well together. If you mix breeds and sizes, they might fight. Try for chickens who grew up together. Leg bands can help you to tell us apart.

Getting ready

Chickens live outdoors, but we'll need a hen house or **coop** to sleep in. We don't like wind, cold or rain! At first, we might need help into our house in bad weather. We like space to move around and stretch. Cover the floor in straw or dry wood shavings for our bedding.

perch

Don't forget the furniture! Chickens need comfortable perches so we can jump up and **roost** at night. Hens like me also need nest boxes where we can lay eggs in peace.

Don't forget to get your garden ready, too! The perfect outdoor space has grass, somewhere to shelter us in bad weather and patches of dry soil. Long blades of grass could get trapped in my tummy, so please keep it mowed.

covered run

Before your chickens come home, check your garden to make sure we can't escape and animals can't get in. Foxes, rats, large birds, and even cats and dogs like to eat us! You'll need fences as tall as a grown-up, or a covered run that can be moved from place to place.

Welcome home

Keep me inside for the first week, so I know it's safe and I don't run away! Show me how to get outdoors and make sure I can find my food and water. Also, give us things to do! We like ropes, wooden blocks or pecking at hanging food.

When we've settled in, we'll love exploring your garden. Watch us carefully, especially with other pets. They might try to eat us! We'll soon learn to go back into our house in the evening to roost. Lock us safely inside for the night. Open the door again in the morning.

Feeding time

Keep feeders full of food made especially for my age and breed. Added **grit** helps me **digest** my food. Chickens scratch at the grass to find seeds and insects to eat. We also eat young roots. Make a game for us by scattering grain in the garden for a treat.

Grit

Chickens drink a lot, so make sure we always have clean, fresh water. We'll need special water bottles in and outside our house. Make sure the water doesn't freeze in cold weather.

Cleaning my home

Help me to stay healthy and clean. Make sure that wild birds and animals can't share my food and water. Check drinkers and feeders every day. Change any stale water, and remember to clear away any food left outside, especially at night.

I like my house to be cleaned once
a week. Scrape dirt and droppings
off perches and boards. Droppings are
a good gift for a grown-up because they
make great **compost**! Put in fresh bedding.
Disinfect all cracks and corners of my home
once a month. Ask for help to choose the
right chemicals to use.

Collecting eggs

Sorry I can't help with the house cleaning. I've been busy laying eggs! We lay up to one egg every day, except when we moult, or shed our feathers. Check my nest box and bedding every morning and evening.

My eggs should be lovely and clean. If you spot droppings on the shells, please clean out my house more often. It could also mean I am sick and need to see the vet. Ask a grown-up to wash and hard boil any dirty eggs.

Time for a bath

Don't worry if you see me rolling around in a cloud of dust. I'm just having a bath! Dust baths help to keep my feathers clean, and free of **mites** and **lice**. Special mite powder helps to do this, too.

If you don't want me to dig holes in your
flowerbeds, make a dust bath. Use a layer of
clean, dry sand or soil in a cat litter tray.
I can use this to have a bath inside my
house when it's raining.

Visiting the vet

If you think I might have mites or lice, take me to visit a vet. The vet can also tell you about **vaccinations** and **worming**. I need worming two or three times a year. Get to know me well so you can tell when I feel poorly.

Signs that I need to visit the vet:

- some feathers are missing or sticking up
- I am bleeding (this could get infected!)
- my head is down and tucked under my wing, or I am trying to look small
- I'm not moving as much as usual
- I'm hiding in a corner
- I have lice or mites, or if they're in my house
- my beak is overgrown or looks odd
- I have a dirty bottom, legs or feet

Holiday care

Holidays are fun for children but not for chickens! We don't like big changes. Ask a friend or neighbour to visit us twice a day. They will need to let us out of our house every morning, give us fresh food and water, and lock us safely inside every evening.

We'll need special care if you need to change our house or food, or if a new chicken comes to live with us. Chicken treats, such as **mealworms** and mixed grains, can help us to settle in. Yum! Now you really are my best friend!

Chicken facts

- Chickens are related to dinosaurs. If you made a family tree for your pet chicken that stretched back millions of years, *Tyrannosaurus rex* would be on it!

- Chickens can't fly very far, but they can flap over a fence or into a tree if they want to. Watch your chickens carefully to make sure they don't escape!

- The red flap on a chicken's head is called a comb.

- Some breeds of chickens lay green or blue eggs.

- A group of chickens is called a flock.

Henrietta's top tips

- Your hens may need to eat oyster shells for extra calcium, a special mineral found in food. They need calcium to lay eggs with strong shells.

- Let town or city officials know you plan to keep chickens on your property, and they will send you information about taking care of your new pets.

- Some towns will even allow you to sell extra eggs! Make sure to check local chicken laws and regulations.

Glossary

breed group of chickens that have the same genetics, size and colour

breeder person who breeds animals

commercial hen hen that lays eggs to sell in shops

compost old plant material or animal droppings used in the garden to help new plants grow

coop cage or pen for keeping chickens

digest break down of food inside the body, so it can be used for energy and growing

disinfect cleaning with chemicals to kill germs

grit tiny stones chickens eat to help break down food

hybrid chicken that has parents of different breeds

lice tiny insects that live on larger animals

mealworm beetle larva used as food for birds

mite tiny spider-like bug that lives on larger animals

roost when birds settle down to rest or sleep

vaccination treatment that prevents an animal from getting a disease

vet person trained to care for ill and injured animals

worming treating an animal with medicines that get rid of worms living inside their body

Find out more

Books

City Chickens, Christine Heppermann
  (HMH Books for Young Readers, 2012)

Squawking Matilda, Lisa Horstman (Two Lions, 2013)

Websites

www.bhwt.org.uk
The British Hen Welfare Trust can help you give a
home to commercial hens. It also has information on
how to care for pet chickens.

**www.rspca.org.uk/allaboutanimals/pets/
farmanimals/chickens**
The website of the RSPCA (Royal Society for the
Prevention of Cruelty to Animals) has information
about pet chickens and how to look after them.

A grown-up can register your chickens online at the
GB Poultry Register
www.gov.uk/poultry-farms-general-regulations.

Index